Welcome to my kitchen.

Nancy Quinn

Nancy Quinn

Cover, writing, recipes, photographs, and book design by Nancy Quinn

Cataloging In Publication Data is available from the publisher upon request.

Copyright 2025 Nancy Quinn. All Rights reserved. No part of this publication may be reproduced or used in any form or by any means, including graphic, electronic, mechanical, photocopying, recording, taping or by any other information and retrieval systems without written permission from the publisher. No AI was used in the creation of this book.

Published by Artist's Quill ISBN: 979-8-9917476-8-4

Printed and bound in the United States of America.

Nancy Quinn's Kitchen

Quick and Easy Sweets and Treats

"Everything Nancy does is quality with love."
Jill Girolamo -Baking Enthusiast

Thank you
for allowing
me to be your
culinary
companion.

Nancy Quinn

This book is dedicated to YOU,

my fellow bakers and readers.

Contents

Introduction 8

Helpful Suggestions 10

When it's time for tea 12

Spring 14

Summer 32

Autumn 54

Winter 68

Christmas 86

Recipe Index 106

Introduction

I am standing in the archway of my kitchen, surveying my domain. Nearly two decades have passed since we left Washington, D.C. to build a new life among the wildlife of a Montana mountainside. So many cherished memories flood me as I look about the room: the bay window over the sink where our horse, Wilson, occasionally spied on me, anxious to sample my latest concoction; the gleaming smooth countertop where high-pitched peals of laughter and little hands covered in dough and frosting helped me prepare cookies; the double stacked oven which regularly scented of homemade bread baking; the glass stovetop with my cherished Pyrex pots rattling as pasta or rice boiled for dinner; the overhead hickory cabinets filled with an eclectic assortment of dinnerware awaiting my selection; and the cleverly hidden mixer which aided me so much when creating such priceless memories as a Nemo birthday cake containing four hundred frosted orange fish scales or an edible "tea set" made from cupcakes with red licorice handles. Like beautiful paintings strategically placed about my kitchen, the memories are always there for me to relive again and again.

As in life, it was not all fun and games. There have been times when the kitchen has been my retreat, a place of solace when life becomes overwhelming. Here I can briefly escape the worldly pressures by creating something comforting for me or by my providing comfort to others. Who doesn't appreciate a steaming cup of tea or hot chocolate? It can be an effective suave for many kinds of wounds. In this sense the kitchen has replaced the hearth as the locus of giving and receiving comfort and joy.

Social media may have supplanted more traditional entertaining, but it is no substitute for face-to-face human interaction, whether it is a simple family get-together or formal dining. This intimate ritual to personally reconnect with each other can range from an ornate teacup to a resplendent table setting. I enjoy having such beauty in my everyday life. Don't you?

To this end I've included some personal stories and tidbits of history about food and spices in this book. Read them for interest and inspiration or go directly to a recipe that piques your curiosity and perhaps later read the accompanying story while enjoying the sweet fragrance wafting from your oven. With so many of my stories connecting our life to the experiments in my kitchen, I'm happily sharing my original recipes for you to make in your own home. I like to think of this book as an opportunity to relate to each other, so I imagine us sitting together over a cup of tea after the kettle has just finished whistling. Consuming treats made by loving hands makes them extra special and offers a feeling of security. The outside world can wait for just awhile longer.

Although the recipes are categorized by seasons, they can be prepared anytime of the year. As time has passed, my creations have become much simpler, my goal being to use ingredients already in the pantry and to create easy and fast treats to delight your eye and palette - with a touch of western elegance. I have labored countless hours to share the best of my efforts with you, and I hope they help you create many wonderful experiences and memories of your own in the years to come. So, gather your favorite baking bowls, utensils, and apron . . . *let's bake!*

Helpful Suggestions

Before I begin preparing a recipe, I read it thoroughly, and check to see if I have all the ingredients in my pantry. I then make sure I understand all the instructions before I begin.

I'm quite generous with my use of vanilla extract, as you will see in these recipes. Try my recommended amounts and I think you will love the result. Pure vanilla extract adds extra flavor to my baked goods. One of my neighbors gave me the nickname the "Vanilla Queen" and I believe it's well earned.

Choose the best ingredients you can source. Real butter is better than margarine or vegetable fats. Any butter with a high fat content, like Amish butter, will give you a more flavorful result. I use pure vanilla extract instead of imitation, and when shopping for chocolate I read the ingredients list. If it contains hydrogenated oils, waxes, or other fillers, I keep looking for a better option. I prefer milk chocolate morsels that contain chocolate liquor, Food Club is a good brand that can be found in many grocery stores.

When using dried fruit, I soak them for a few minutes in a few tablespoons of hot water or rum, depending on the recipe, before I mix them into the dough.

Don't overmix the butter and sugar when you are creaming them together. It will cause the butter to separate and will change the texture of your recipe, hindering your effort. If you don't have time to soften the butter, try shredding it on a box grater.

I use a nonstick baking pan lined with parchment paper. It helps prevent burning and you'll be rewarded with nice lightly browned edges and bottoms to your cookies. Clean up is quick and easy, too.

Cooling racks are not expensive and are worth using instead of leaving the cookies to cool on the baking sheets or on paper towels. The racks provide much needed air circulation and prevent the risk of your baked goods drying out as they will continue to cook slightly if left on a hot baking pan.

Many recipes require room temperature ingredients. If you need to warm your eggs, place them in a cup of tepid water for a few minutes.

Make sure you use the correct pan size recommended in the recipe. The wrong baking pan can result in a change of texture and cooking times for my recipes.

When preparing citrus cookies or cakes, mix a little of the zest with the sugar before creaming it with the butter.

Remember to preheat your oven before you start baking.

To avoid flat cookies caused by the dough spreading out too much in the oven, I often refrigerate it for a half hour before I drop the cookies onto the pans. The cold dough will keep its shape during baking.

I have a collection of colorful dishtowels that I enjoy using and they are a fun addition to my time in the kitchen. The one featured below always cheers me up and makes me smile.

When it's time for tea . . .

According to legend, in 2737 BC the Chinese emperor Shen Nung was sitting beneath a tree while his servant was boiling water for them to drink. At some point during this process a few of the leaves fell into the pot. This is the story of the origin of drinking tea.

The tea time ritual in England was begun in the 1740s by the Seventh Duchess of Bedford. It was fashionable at that time to serve the evening meal as late as 8pm. The Duchess became hungry in the late afternoon and often retreated to her bedchamber to secretly consume tea with bread, butter, and cake. Over time she began inviting her friends to join her and a new tradition was born. It is still considered an honor for a close friend to join you for tea in the privacy of your bedroom.

Today you don't have to sit under a tree or withdraw to your bedroom to have the perfect cup of tea. Cold running water straight from the tap is fully oxygenated and a good starting point for the brewing process. I use an old-fashioned kettle that whistles when the water boils. I also have an electric countertop kettle. While waiting for the kettle to boil, fill the serving vessel of your choice and the tea cups with hot tap water to warm them. Discard this water before serving the tea. Ideally, I think tea tastes best out of a porcelain pot and cup, but I often pour the tea directly into a ceramic mug if I don't have time to sit at leisure.

The rule of thumb when preparing a pot of tea is to add to the empty serving pot one teaspoon of loose tea for each planned cup plus one extra teaspoon. This rule applies to tea bags as well. Next, as soon as the water boils, pour it into the serving pot (or teacup). If the water boils too long, its flavor actually changes. Allow the tea to steep for the time indicated on the packaging, usually no more than 5 minutes. If it is left too long in the hot water, tannins are released and the tea becomes bitter. I must admit I'm an impatient American and have been known to dunk the tea bag in and out of the cup. I've even seen others commit the unpardonable sin of squeezing the bag! However, I draw the line at stirring the tea with my spoon and clanking it on the cup, so there is yet hope for me.

China Markings

If there is no mark on the underside of your china, the piece was made before 1891. This was before the United States required imported pieces to indicate the country of origin. China labeled with only the country were likely made from 1891-1914.

Luscious Lemon Bars

Crust:

1 cup flour plus two tablespoons

½ cup butter, softened

¼ cup confectioners' sugar

1 teaspoon lemon extract

1 teaspoon grated lemon peel

2 tablespoons lemon juice (lemon pulp is optional)

Filling:

2 eggs

1 cup sugar

2 tablespoons flour

½ teaspoon baking powder

2 tablespoons lemon juice

¼ teaspoon lemon extract

1 teaspoon grated lemon peel

Preheat oven to 350°F.

Crust: In a bowl combine the flour, butter, and confectioners' sugar. Then add the lemon extract, lemon peel, and lemon juice. Mix and pat into an ungreased 8-inch x 8-inch baking dish. Bake at 350°F for 20 minutes.

Filling: In a mixing bowl beat eggs and sugar together, then add the flour, baking powder, lemon juice, and lemon extract. Beat until mixture is frothy. Mix in lemon peel and pour over the crust. Bake for 25 minutes or until golden brown. Cool on a wire rack and dust with confectioners' sugar. Cut into squares and enjoy!

Lemons are native to Asia and are a hybrid between the sour orange and a citron.

In the past lemons were considered a status symbol of wealth or royalty.

They were often given as a token of goodwill.

A lemon tree can produce up to 600 pounds of lemons a year.

Chocolate Almond Bars

10 minutes to make, nothing to bake!

1 and ¼ cups of Brownie Brittle (graham crackers or chocolate wafer style cookies are another option)

½ cup almond butter

½ cup melted butter

1 and ½ cups of confectioners' sugar

1 cup of real milk chocolate chips

Grind Brownie Brittle (it can be found in many grocery stores) or cookies in a chopper or food processor and mix it with the almond butter, melted butter, and confectioner's sugar. Stir together until it's mixed into a paste. Pat the mixture into an 8-inch x 8-inch or 9-inch x 9-inch pan.

Melt the chocolate until smooth and spread on top of your almond mixture. Refrigerate for about 15 - 20 minutes and then cut into desired shapes. Use straight cuts for bars or diagonal cuts if you prefer diamond shaped cookies.

Return to the refrigerator and keep them cold. It will take at least an hour for them to completely set. They can be frozen or stored in the refrigerator for a week or so, if they last that long!

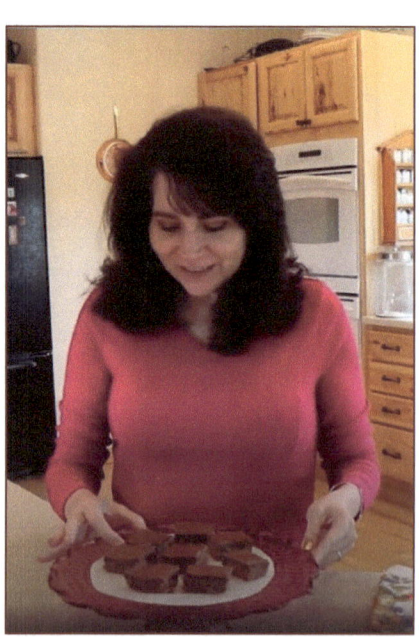

Cinnamon Honey Butter

½ cup butter, softened

¼ cup confectioners' sugar

1 tablespoon honey

1 and 1/2 teaspoons vanilla extract

¼ teaspoon of ground cinnamon

Mix these ingredients until well blended and store in the refrigerator. I like to keep it in a glass jar or pretty decanter with a lid. This is a real treat on toast, waffles, biscuits, or other baked goods such as cornbread and flour tortillas.

Pumpkin Waffles

2 cups Krusteaz mix (Bisquick or Pioneer Mix are other choices)

1 cup powdered milk

2 cups water

1 teaspoon vanilla extract

½ to 1 tablespoon ground cinnamon

2 eggs stiffly beaten

2 tablespoons canola oil

1 cup canned pumpkin

Mix together the Krusteaz, powdered milk, and water.

Add the vanilla extract, cinnamon, eggs, canola oil, and pumpkin.

Combine well and pour batter into a waffle iron and cook.

Pumpkin recipes in the spring? Yes! These waffles are perfect for brunch, a leisurely Sunday morning, or for a special occasion. They are often our choice for Easter breakfast.

I've been making this cornbread for decades. My first attempt at this recipe was in my tiny kitchen in Florida when I was a teenager. I loved the addition of the maple syrup. Who knew it would also be popular in Montana! This sweet golden cornbread is meant to be enjoyed in any area of the country - or the world!

Did you know the world record for the largest corn plant is 48 feet tall?

Go West, Southern Cornbread!

1 and ¼ cups flour

¾ cup of cornmeal

½ cup sugar

2 teaspoons baking powder

½ teaspoon salt

1 cup milk

1 cup vegetable oil

1 egg

¼ cup maple syrup

Preheat oven to 400°F and spray an 8-inch x 8-inch pan with nonstick oil. Mix together flour, cornmeal, sugar, baking powder, and salt. Then add the milk, vegetable oil, egg, and maple syrup. Stir well until combined. Pour into pan and bake 25 minutes or until golden brown on top.

Easy Wagon Wheel Flour Tortillas

2 cups flour plus one tablespoon

1 teaspoon salt

1 teaspoon baking powder

4 tablespoons melted butter

¾ cup of warm water

In a large mixing bowl stir in the flour, salt, and baking powder. Add the melted butter and begin mixing as you slowly add the water. Make sure it is well incorporated, then knead the dough for a minute or two.

Shape it into a ball and divide the dough into eight equal pieces. Roll each piece into an approximately 8-inch circle or use a tortilla press.

Heat your ungreased skillet or griddle to about 375°F and cook the tortillas for a minute or two on each side. You'll know to turn them over when the tortillas begin to bubble slightly and brown. Place on a cooling rack.

Decadent Éclair Cake

Topping:

1 stick butter

1 cup granulated sugar

1/3 cup cocoa

¼ cup low-fat milk

1 teaspoon vanilla extract

1/8 teaspoon salt

Batter:

2 boxes instant sugar free vanilla pudding mix

3 cups milk

8 ounces nondairy whipped topping (Cool Whip) or homemade whipped cream (add ½ teaspoon of vanilla extract to whipped cream)

Shell:

Cinnamon graham crackers

Prepare your topping first. Melt butter in a saucepan and add sugar, cocoa, and milk. Stir while bringing to a boil. Cook for one minute. Remove from heat. Add vanilla extract and salt. Let mixture cool.

Mix your pudding and milk, then fold in the nondairy topping or whipped cream.

In an 8-inch x 11-inch pan or glass dish put in a layer of graham crackers. Spread half of the batter on the crackers. Place a second layer of crackers on top and lay in the rest of the batter. Add a third layer of graham crackers to the top of this and cover completely with the chocolate topping. Refrigerate for three to four hours - overnight is even better.

This is a real treat. When my husband and I were dating, he prepared dinner for us one evening and served this fabulous dessert. He even cleared the table and insisted on cleaning the kitchen himself!

Carrot Cake

4 eggs

2 cups sugar

1 and ½ cups vegetable oil

2 cups all-purpose flour

3 teaspoons ground cinnamon

1 teaspoon baking powder

1 teaspoon baking soda

1/4 teaspoon of salt

¼ teaspoon of ground nutmeg

2 cups finely grated carrots or pureed carrots- baby food in the jar makes a moist cake

Frosting:

2 tablespoons butter, softened

8-ounce package cream cheese, softened

3 cups confectioners' sugar (you may need more than this for consistency)

2 teaspoons vanilla extract

2 tablespoons milk

Preheat oven to 350°F and in a mixing bowl combine the eggs, sugar, and oil, mixing well. Combine flour, cinnamon, baking powder, baking soda, salt, and nutmeg. Beat into the mixture, then stir in the carrots.

Pour into two greased and floured 9-inch round cake pans and bake for 30 to 40 minutes or until a toothpick inserted near the center comes out clean. Cool before removing from your pans to cooling racks.

To prepare the frosting, in a mixing bowl cream the butter and cream cheese, add confectioners' sugar and vanilla extract with enough milk to achieve your desired consistency. Spread between layers and on top of the cake. The leftovers should be refrigerated.

Crème De Menthe Brownies

Preheat oven to 350°F.

Mix below ingredients and bake in a 13-inch x 9-inch pan for 30 minutes.

1 cup sugar

1/2 cup butter

4 beaten eggs

1 cup flour

½ teaspoon salt

16 ounces of chocolate syrup

2 teaspoons vanilla extract

Set aside and let cool

> Crème De Menthe is French for "mint cream" it's a fragrant, sweet, mint flavored alcoholic beverage.

Cream together the three ingredients below and spread on top of the brownies:

2 cups confectioners' sugar

½ cup butter

2 tablespoons Crème De Menthe (I prefer the green for presentation, but clear works. The color comes from mint leaves or extract and can be processed out)

The last step is to melt together the two ingredients below, let cool, and pour over brownies:

1 cup milk chocolate or semi-sweet chips

6 tablespoons butter

This is the perfect marriage of chocolate and mint. Since I have a chocolate mint plant growing in my greenhouse, I often harvest a few sprigs and use them as a garnish on top of these brownies.

Fresh Blueberry Cookies

1 cup butter, softened

1 cup granulated sugar

¾ cup brown sugar

2 eggs

2 tablespoons vanilla extract

2 cups all-purpose flour

1 cup almond flour

1 teaspoon salt

½ teaspoon baking soda

2 cups fresh blueberries

Preheat oven to 350°F.

Line baking sheets with parchment paper.

In a mixer cream butter and both sugars until light and fluffy.

Mix in eggs and vanilla extract.

In a separate bowl combine the all-purpose flour, almond flour, salt, and baking soda until it's well incorporated. Mix this into the batter.

With a spoon or spatula gently stir in the fresh blueberries. Be very careful, otherwise the blueberries will break up and turn your batter a bluish gray color which is undesirable.

Place a generous teaspoon of dough approximately two inches apart on your baking sheet and bake for 12 - 14 minutes.

Remove from the cookie sheet after a few minutes and cool on racks. Store in the refrigerator.

"The blueberry cookies are a bite from heaven!!" Michael Hoard- Cookie Connoisseur

In the past blueberries were called "star berries" because the blossom end of the berry resembles a five-pointed star.

Better Batter Pecan Cake

1 cup butter, softened

2 cups sugar

4 eggs

½ cup finely ground pecans

1 and ½ tablespoons vanilla extract

1 cup sour cream

1 and ¼ cups milk

2 and ½ cups cake flour

½ teaspoon baking soda

1/2 teaspoon salt

Glaze:

½ cup melted butter

2 cups confectioners' sugar

1 tablespoon vanilla extract

The glaze recipe is handy for use on other baked goods such as cookies and doughnuts.

Preheat oven to 350°F.

Grease a 10-inch Bundt pan or cake pan.

With a mixer, cream the butter and sugar until fluffy. Beat in the eggs and pecans, combining well, then add vanilla extract.

Combine sour cream and milk, add them to the batter and beat well.

In a separate bowl combine flour, baking soda, and salt, then add to the mixer and beat well. Pour this into a pan and bake for about 60 minutes.

To prepare the glaze melt ½ cup butter and add two cups confectioners' sugar and one tablespoon of vanilla extract. Add a spoonful or two of hot water to reach desired consistency. Incorporate well and pour over cake.

The Pecan Cake Fiasco

I remember collecting pecans that fell onto the ground when I was a teenager living in Florida. I would sit in the kitchen and remove the shells, admiring their perfect shape while chopping and grinding them. I always saved several cartons in the freezer for use in future concoctions.

As a grown woman I still like pecans and use them in many of my recipes. However, now that I live in Montana I must buy them in bulk from the grocery store. I had just purchased a new bag of pecans and wanted to use some of them while they were still fresh, so I had a pecan cake baking in the oven. It was a perfect spring day outside. The birds happily chirped and sang in the trees behind the house and our horse, Wilson, grazed nearby in full view from our dining room window. The scene was so enchanting that it occurred to me the best way to enjoy this dessert would be on our back patio after lunch.

As I was setting the table I once more glanced out the window, only to see Wilson had now moved to the edge of the patio. He was clearly agitated because he was snorting, backing up, and charging forward at the nearby tree line. I surveyed the area, looking for the cause of his behavior. Then I saw it, a large dark shape emerging from the outer bushes.

"Bill," I yelled, "there's a bear near the dining room and Wilson is out there with him!" Upon hearing my outburst, my youngest daughter, Sonja, sprang outside in her stocking feet to save her horse. "Sonja," I called, "come back inside!" She ignored my command and the danger, so I immediately chased after her. Bill must have heard me because he came rushing down the stairs with a rifle and followed me.

The bear, fully aware of all this commotion, decided he wanted no part of our circus and moved back into the woods. We calmed Wilson and I scolded Sonja about her reckless action. It was only after I had finished counseling her that I smelled a burning odor. My cake! I rushed to retrieve it from our smoking oven, but was too late. It was completely scorched and inedible and I was too tired to start over, so we settled for ice cream sundaes as dessert - inside at the dining room table.

Hopefully, you won't have to deal with bears when you make this cake, but I think this moist cake brimming with vanilla is worth the risk.

Our horse, Whiskey, seen on the previous page, loved to nibble these roses. Because he was 35 years old, I allowed him this pleasure.

This little gal is a regular visitor to my garden, and is one of the reasons we have a green house.

Chocolate Brownies

1 and ¼ cups sugar

2 eggs

1 and 1/2 teaspoons vanilla extract

3 tablespoons chocolate syrup

½ cup melted butter

½ cup flour

1 cup baking cocoa

1/4 teaspoon baking powder

¼ teaspoon salt

Optional: ¼ cup of chopped walnuts or pecans

Frosting:

3 tablespoons baking cocoa

3 tablespoons melted butter

2 tablespoons vanilla extract

1 and ½ cups confectioners' sugar

Preheat oven to 350°F.

In a large mixing bowl, beat sugar, eggs, vanilla extract, and chocolate syrup; add butter and mix well.

In a separate bowl combine flour, cocoa, baking powder, and salt, then add to batter and mix well. You can add chopped nuts if desired.

Pour into a greased 8-inch x 8-inch baking pan and bake for 25 - 30 minutes or until a toothpick inserted near the center comes out clean. Cool on a wire rack.

To prepare the frosting combine cocoa, butter, and vanilla extract, then gradually stir in confectioners' sugar. Add water or milk to thin as needed so it will spread smoothly over the brownies.

Leopard Bark

The organic patterns on the coat of a clouded leopard have been etched in my mind for decades. I like my baked creations to look as wonderful as they taste, so I was inspired to create this recipe. I reproduced the pattern by painting dark chocolate into white chocolate. It's easy and delicious!

8 ounces chopped white chocolate

8 ounces chopped milk chocolate

Line a cookie sheet with parchment paper.

Melt chocolates separately, but at the same time. For double boilers, use simmering water until the chocolates become easy to stir. Another method is to place them in glass bowls and microwave them in 15 second intervals to avoid scorching. Whichever method you use, don't overcook the chocolates or they won't spread properly.

Pour white chocolate onto cookie sheet and spread evenly. Place a large teaspoon of milk chocolate on top of the white and gently pull it across to form an oval. Drag the milk chocolate into thinner stripes and dots. Let it cool before breaking it into pieces. It will be a tasty work of art.

Book is available online and in stores (Leopard bark not included)

Favorite Strawberry Refrigerated Jam

This is an easy jam recipe that must be kept in the refrigerator for no more than two weeks or in a freezer for approximately four months. No canning skills are required.

4 cups chopped strawberries

1 cup sugar

2 tablespoon lime or lemon juice

Put stove top burner on high

Place all ingredients in a pot and bring to a boil.

Reduce heat to medium high and cook at a low rolling boil for 15 minutes or until thick consistency is achieved.

Remove from heat. As it cools it will continue to thicken.

Place in glass containers with lids and store in refrigerator or freezer.

It's delicious as a traditional jam, but also wonderful on ice cream!

Ice Cream Cookies

1 cup butter

¾ cup sugar

2 cups all-purpose flour

¼ teaspoon salt

1 tablespoon vanilla extract

2 generous tablespoons vanilla ice cream

Preheat oven 300°F.

In a mixer, cream the butter and sugar, gradually add in flour and salt, and then mix in vanilla extract and ice cream.

Roll dough into a cylindrical shape about 1 and ½ inches in diameter. Tap each end with the bottom of a glass to eliminate any taper. Seal the dough in plastic wrap and refrigerate until firm (about 45 minutes or overnight if desired).

Slice the dough every 1/4 inch or slightly thicker, depending on your preference, and place on ungreased baking sheets.

Bake for 40 - 50 minutes until edges are slightly brown.

I chose vanilla ice cream for this recipe, but it's fun to use different flavors such as pistachio or cherry, or choose any of the interesting custom flavors found in your local grocery store.

Dipped Vanilla Cookies

¾ cup butter, softened

½ cup confectioners' sugar

3 teaspoons vanilla extract

½ teaspoon salt

1 and ½ cups all-purpose flour

Preheat oven to 325°F.

In a mixer, beat butter at a medium speed until creamy. Add confectioners' sugar, vanilla extract, and salt, then beat until it's smooth. Gradually add flour and combine well.

If you would like to use the roll and slice method, roll dough into a cylindrical shape about 1 and ½ inches in diameter. Tap each end with the bottom of a glass to eliminate any taper. Seal the dough in plastic wrap and refrigerate until firm (about 30- 45 minutes).

If you prefer to cut out shapes, place the dough on plastic wrap and press into a disc shape, seal, and refrigerate for 20 minutes.

Line baking sheets with parchment paper.

Place the cylindrical dough on a lightly floured board or counter and cut into ½ inch slices. For disc shaped dough, roll to ¼ inch thickness. Use cookie cutters to form desired shapes and transfer them to cookie sheets.

Bake for 10 - 15 minutes. Let cool on a wire rack.

White chocolate ganache:

8 ounces finely chopped white chocolate

1 tablespoon of butter, softened

¼ cup heavy whipping cream

Place ingredients in a glass bowl and microwave at 15 second intervals.

Stir well between each heat cycle until mixture is smooth. Dip each cookie into warm ganache and let set until coating is hardened and cooled.

Banana Bread

½ cup butter

1 cup sugar

2 eggs

1 and 1/2 to 2 cups mashed ripe banana (very ripe is best)

¼ cup sour cream

3 tablespoons vanilla extract

2 cups flour

1 teaspoon baking powder

½ teaspoon baking soda

¼ teaspoon salt

1 or 2 tablespoons milk

Optional: ½ cup ground or chopped nuts (my husband's preference)

Preheat oven to 350°F.

Line a 5-inch x 9-inch loaf pan or 8-inch x 8-inch baking dish with parchment paper on the bottom. Coat with non-stick cooking spray.

In a mixer, cream the butter and sugar. Add eggs, banana, sour cream, and vanilla extract to the mixture and stir on low. In a separate bowl combine the flour, baking powder, baking soda, and salt. Add this to the mixer and continue stirring on low. If the batter looks too thick, add a tablespoon or two of milk.

Spoon the batter into the pan and bake for 50 - 55 minutes. I put my cake pan on a cookie sheet in the oven to help prevent scorching the bottom of the cake.

The bananas we eat today are a different variety from those that were originally cultivated for thousands of years.

In the 1950s the Cavendish banana was the most common plant grown and distributed. When the crops fell to a widespread fungus known as Panama Disease, it caused a banana shortage. This was referred to as the banana blight, and it forced growers to switch to more disease resistant plants. It was a costly endeavor for the banana industry and consumers alike. Sometimes I wonder what the original bananas tasted like, but I'm happy we still have this fruit to enjoy. (Note: Contrary to popular belief, the blight did not inspire the popular song *Yes! We Have No Bananas*, which was written in 1923 by Frank Silver and Irving Cohn.)

Life-Changing Cookies

½ cup room temperature butter

½ cup brown sugar

1 cup flour

¼ teaspoon baking soda

1/8 teaspoon salt

1 cup oats

¾ cup or more of fruit spread (I have used apricot, cherry, blueberry, and strawberry)

Preheat oven to 350°F.

Butter an 8-inch x 8-inch pan or line it with parchment paper.

Mix all ingredients except the jam. Press a little more than half of this mixture into the bottom of the pan and pat firmly. Spread in the jam almost to the edges. Crumble the rest of the oat mix on top, lightly pressing it into the jam.

Bake for 30 - 40 minutes and allow to cool on a wire rack before cutting.

I have been making these bar cookies since I was a teenager and I'm constantly asked for the recipe. It has opened the door to new friendships and is always a favorite at potluck suppers. It also makes a delicious gift, especially when it's wrapped in a pretty box or presented on a lovely plate. Who knows, it may even inspire a marriage proposal or two!

Easy Pizza Dough

1 and ½ cups warm water

2 and ½ teaspoons rapid rise yeast

2 teaspoons sugar

1 and ½ teaspoons salt

2 tablespoons olive oil

½ teaspoon granulated garlic

3 to 4 cups bread flour

In a mixer bowl, whisk water and yeast and let stand for a few minutes to allow the yeast to dissolve. Whisk in sugar, salt, oil, garlic, and three cups of bread flour. Mix to make a soft mass, add extra flour if dough looks to wet. Install a dough hook on the lowest speed and form a soft smoother elastic dough. This takes about 6 - 7 minutes. Alternately, you can do this part by hand, kneading the dough.

Coat your dough with olive oil and cover it in a bowl with Saran Wrap over the top. Allow the dough to rise until almost double in size. This can take up to 90 minutes.

Drizzle pizza pans or baking sheets with olive oil.

Remove dough and handle it to fit into prepared pans. Drizzle a little more olive oil on top. Spread on your favorite sauces and toppings.

Preheat oven to 425°F and bake 15 minutes. Reduce oven temperature to 400°F and continue baking until toppings are lightly browned.

Bourbon Pecan Pie

1 and 1/8 cup brown sugar

¼ cup butter

½ teaspoon salt

3 eggs

½ cup white corn syrup

1 teaspoon vanilla extract

1 ounce bourbon

¼ pound pecan halves

Preheat oven to at 350°F

Beat sugar, butter, and salt well. Add eggs and beat only until mixed.

Blend in corn syrup, vanilla extract, and bourbon. Arrange the pecans in bottom of crust (from recipe below or use a store-bought crust), and pour mixture on top.

Bake for 30 - 40 minutes. Do not over bake. The center should still look uncooked or jiggly. Remove and allow to cool on a trivet until solid.

Single Pie Crust:

1 and ¼ cups flour

1/2 teaspoon salt

½ cup butter

4 tablespoons water

In a bowl stir together flour and salt. Cut in butter, sprinkle some water, mix, and add more water, mixing until dough forms a soft ball. On a lightly floured surface roll out dough into a circle and place in a pie dish.

Chocolate Chip Cookies

2 and 1/4 cups flour

1 teaspoon baking soda

1 teaspoon salt

¾ cup packed brown sugar

¾ cup sugar

¾ cup butter

1 egg

4 teaspoons vanilla extract (one of my nicknames is Vanilla Queen)

3 or 4 tablespoons milk

¾ cup real milk chocolate chips

¾ cups semi-sweet chocolate chips

Preheat oven to 325°F.

Combine the flour, baking soda, and salt in a bowl and set aside.

Cream the sugars and butter in a mixer until a grainy paste forms.

Add in the egg, vanilla extract, and milk until incorporated.

Slowly add the flour combination to the mixer, then drop in all the chocolate chips, stirring until just blended.

Drop by tablespoons about two inches apart onto an ungreased baking sheet or one lined with parchment paper.

Bake for about 14 minutes. Remove cookies from sheet and cool them on wire racks. Depending on their size, this recipe yields 24 – 60 cookies.

These cookies are great with a cold glass of milk, or a scoop of ice cream between two cookies makes a tasty sandwich. My family is never far from the kitchen when these cookies are in the oven.

Cookies and Conversation

A fistful of wildflowers

The slam of the screen door

The table set for tea

A lace napkin hits the floor

But those days are gone, they won't happen anymore

For my girls are grown and now I'm alone

Oh, how I long for cookies and conversation

Little tears in the night

A tiny hand in mind

Hold on to Mommy, everything is fine

Lullabies that linger in my mind

Checking for monsters under the bed

These images live in my heart and head

Remembering lingering hugs and smiles

Skinned knees and honey bees, handmade paper dolls

Now these are only memories

But those days are gone, they won't happen anymore

For my girls are grown and now I'm alone

Oh, how I long for cookies and conversation copyright 2025

Some of you may know I was a professional vocalist and wrote my own songs many years ago. I often have a tune in mind when words come to me. I penned these lyrics entitled "Cookies and Conversation" one afternoon standing at my kitchen counter. Later, when I read them out loud to my precious pup, Penny, her look gave me genuine comfort and made me smile.

Cinnamon Oatmeal Cookies

1 and ¼ cups butter, softened

¾ cup packed brown sugar

½ cup granulated sugar

1 egg

1 tablespoon vanilla extract

½ cup all-purpose flour

1 teaspoon baking soda

2 teaspoons ground cinnamon

1/2 teaspoon of salt

¼ teaspoon ground nutmeg

3 cups oats

Preheat oven to 375°F.

In a mixing bowl beat butter and sugars until creamy.

Add egg and vanilla extract and beat well.

Combine in a separate bowl the flour, baking soda, cinnamon, salt, and nutmeg, mixing them well. Add the oats. Incorporate into batter.

Drop generous tablespoons of dough onto ungreased cookie sheets.

Bake for 8 - 9 minutes.

When slightly cooled remove cookies from the baking sheets and place them on wire cooling racks. Depending on their size, this recipe can yield 24 – 60 cookies.

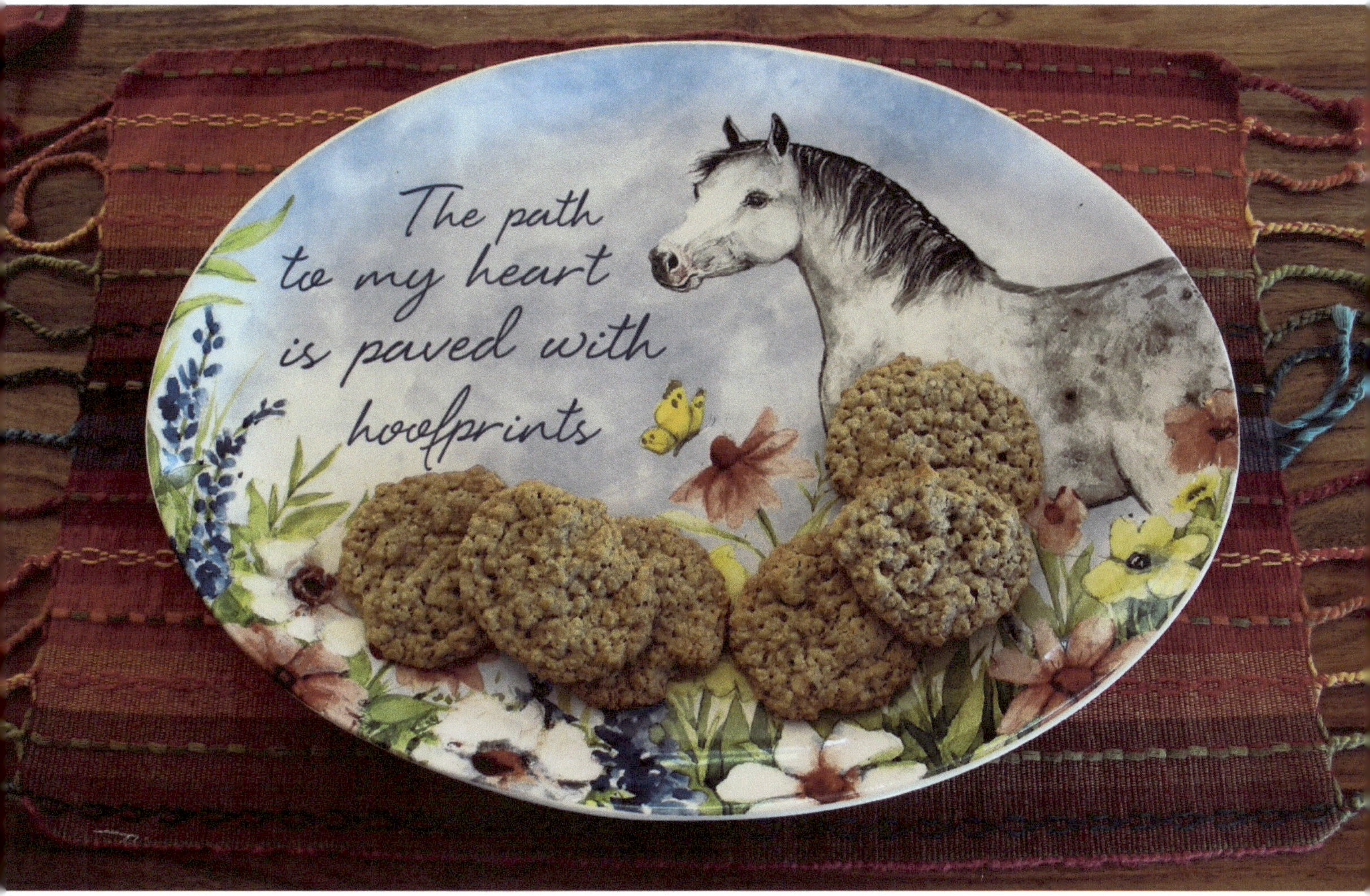
The path
to my heart
is paved with
hoofprints

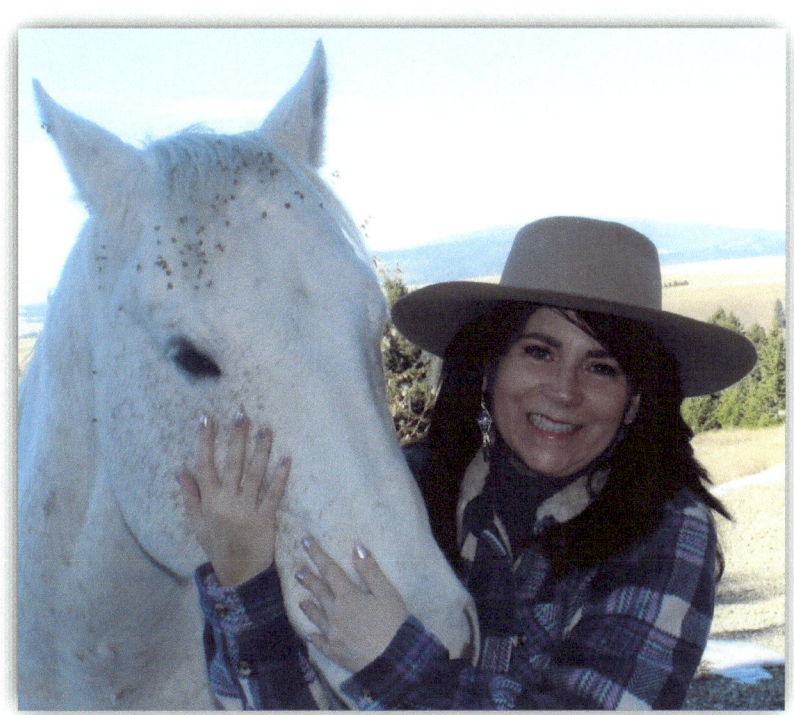

Pumpkin Spice

Pumpkin spice is a combination of cinnamon, ginger, nutmeg, and cloves. Its history begins in Ceylon where cinnamon originates. It is believed to be the first trade spice, with evidence dating its use in China to 2800 BC. It migrated to India, and from there reached Europe in 2000 BC, arriving through overland trade routes. Its scarcity and popularity made it equal to ivory and gold in value; thus, its origin was purposely shrouded in mystery and fantasy until 1505 when Portuguese traders discovered Ceylon. Six years later they discovered Indonesia, where on the "Spice Islands" (Maluku) nutmeg, mace, and cloves were being grown. For the next three centuries the Spice Islands, along with Ceylon, were the focus of both trade wars and real wars among succeeding colonial powers, including Portugal, Spain, the Netherlands, and England. These spices migrated to the American colonies and became popular blends for cooking an American original, the pumpkin pie. Despite the pie's popularity, the spices had to be hand-ground and mixed in proper proportions. By the early 20th century this time-consuming practice was threating the spice industry, so in 1933 the Thompson & Taylor Spice Company offered the first pre-blended pumpkin pie spice, consisting of nine spices. In 1934 McCormick & Company introduced their simpler pumpkin spice made of cinnamon, ginger, nutmeg, and allspice, which is still available today.

Pumpkin Bread

1 and ½ cups sugar

1 and ¼ cups flour

1 teaspoon baking soda

¼ teaspoon baking powder

½ teaspoon or more, ground cinnamon

1/4 teaspoon or more, ground nutmeg

1 cup canned pumpkin

½ cup vegetable oil

1/3 cup water

2 eggs

Preheat oven to 350°F.

Mix dry ingredients in a bowl, and combine them with pumpkin, oil, water, and eggs.

Pour into a greased loaf pan or 9-inch x 9-inch baking pan.

Bake for about 45- 50 minutes (baking time may increase with a loaf pan). Insert a toothpick in the center. If it comes out dry it is ready for cooling on a trivet.

It's my personal tradition to bake this bread
on the first cool day of the year.

Pumpkin Cheesecake

Crust:

1 and 1/3 cups cinnamon graham cracker crumbs

¼ cup melted butter

Filling:

3 packages (8 ounces each) cream cheese, softened

¾ cup sugar

½ cup packed brown sugar

3 eggs

1 can (15 ounces) solid pack pumpkin

4 teaspoons vanilla extract

1 teaspoon ground cinnamon

¼ teaspoon ground nutmeg

Preheat oven to 350°F.

Combine cracker crumbs and butter, press into the bottom and one inch up the sides of a greased 10-inch springform pan.

In a mixing bowl beat cream cheese and sugars until smooth.

Add eggs, beating until just combined. Add pumpkin, vanilla extract, cinnamon, and nutmeg. Stir just until blended.

Pour onto crust and place on a baking sheet.

Bake for 60 - 65 minutes or until center is nearly set. Chill overnight in the refrigerator. Carefully remove the sides of the pan. I free the edges with a knife beforehand.

Milk Chocolate Chunk Cookies

½ cup granulated sugar

½ cup packed brown sugar

½ cup butter, softened

2 eggs

1 teaspoon vanilla extract

1 and ¾ cups all-purpose flour

½ cup unsweetened Dutch cocoa

1 teaspoon baking soda

¼ teaspoon salt

1 cup milk chocolate chips

Preheat oven to 375°F.

In a large mixing bowl combine the sugars, butter, eggs, and vanilla extract.

Using a mixer beat at medium speed until blended.

In a separate bowl combine flour, cocoa, baking soda, and salt. Slowly add this to the mixing bowl while beating at low speed until a soft dough forms. Stir in the chocolate chips.

Drop heaping tablespoons of dough spaced about three inches apart on two ungreased cookie sheets.

Bake for 8 - 10 minutes or until set. Let pans cool for a minute or two on trivets before removing the cookies to cooling racks. This recipe makes about two dozen cookies.

These cookies make an afternoon tea break much sweeter.

Montana Gold Bars

Crust:

2/3 cup confectioners' sugar

2 cups all-purpose flour

1 cup butter, softened

Topping:

2/3 cup melted butter

½ cup honey

3 tablespoons milk

2 teaspoons vanilla extract

½ cup packed brown sugar

2 and ½ cups cashews

Grind the nuts in a chopper, but do not turn into paste.

Preheat oven to 350°F.

Butter a 9-inch x 13-inch baking pan.

In a bowl add confectioners' sugar and flour, mix in the softened butter until mixture is combined. Pat firmly into the bottom of the pan.

Bake for 20 minutes.

While the crust is baking, in a medium sized bowl combine melted butter, honey, milk, vanilla extract, and brown sugar. Mix just until blended and stir in the cashews.

Spread topping over the hot crust and bake for an additional 25 minutes. The center will be bubbling. Cool on a trivet and cut into bars. Refrigerate or freeze leftovers in an airtight container.

My little tribute to the beautiful state of Montana.

Vanilla Cranberry Muffins

1 cup butter, softened

1 and ¾ cup sugar

4 eggs

2 tablespoons vanilla extract

4 cups all-purpose flour

4 teaspoons baking powder

½ teaspoon baking soda

1/2 teaspoon salt

¼ teaspoon ground cinnamon

1 cup sour cream

½ cup milk

1 and 1/2 cups chopped fresh cranberries

Preheat oven to 400°F.

Spray muffin cups with a nonstick cooking spray or use paper cupcake liners. (This recipe works for the extra-large muffins as well.)

With a mixer, blend butter and sugar, add eggs and vanilla extract, and blend until smooth.

In a separate bowl combine flour, baking powder, baking soda, salt, and cinnamon. Add to mixer. Blend in sour cream and milk. Turn off mixer and add cranberries in by hand.

Place batter into each muffin cup and bake for approximately 20 minutes until muffins are gently browned. Cool a few minutes before removing from pan.

Presentation Pumpkin Cake

2 cups granulated sugar

1 cup of melted butter

4 eggs

16 ounces solid pack pumpkin

1 teaspoon vanilla extract

2 cups all-purpose flour

1 tablespoon ground cinnamon

2 teaspoons baking powder

1 teaspoon baking soda

1 teaspoon ground ginger

½ teaspoon ground nutmeg

¾ teaspoon salt

Glaze

½ cup melted butter

2 cups confectioners' sugar

1 tablespoon vanilla extract

Preheat oven to 350°F.

Combine sugar, butter, eggs, pumpkin and vanilla, in a mixing bowl and beat well.

In a separate bowel combine flour, cinnamon, baking powder, baking soda, ginger, nutmeg, and salt. Add to pumpkin mixture while beating at low speed until blended. Pour into greased or buttered bundt pan.

Bake for 40 - 50 minutes or until a toothpick inserted in the center comes out clean. Cool before removing from pan.

To prepare glaze, melt butter. Incorporate confectioners' sugar and vanilla extract. If needed, add a tablespoon of hot water. Pour over cake.

Cinnamon Swirl Donut Bread

2 cups flour

1 cup sugar

1 teaspoon baking soda

½ teaspoon salt

¾ cup milk

¼ cup heavy cream

1 large egg

¼ cup canola oil

1 tablespoon vanilla extract

1 and ½ tablespoons ground cinnamon

½ cup sugar

Preheat oven to 350°F.

In a large bowl, combine flour, one cup sugar, baking soda, and salt.

Combine milk, cream, egg, oil, and vanilla extract, then mix with dry ingredients just until moistened.

In a small bowl combine cinnamon and remaining sugar.

Grease a 9-inch x 5-inch loaf pan and pour half of the batter in it.

Sprinkle with ¾ of the cinnamon sugar mixture. Carefully spread remaining batter on top, then sprinkle with the leftover cinnamon sugar.

With a butter knife cut through the batter in a swirling motion.

Bake about 45 - 50 minutes. Place on a trivet to cool before removing bread from the pan to cool completely on a wire rack.

This is much easier to make than a donut. It's perfect for a snack or served with breakfast. It's moist and packed full of cinnamon.

Hot Toddy

Boiling water as needed

2 ounces scotch, bourbon, rye, Irish whiskey, or dark rum.

1 and ½ tablespoons honey

3-inch lemon peel

1 cinnamon stick

Fill a mug or glass with boiling water and set aside for one minute.

Pour out the water then add the spirit and honey to the warmed glass.

Top with boiling water and stir until the honey is dissolved.

Garnish with the lemon peel and cinnamon stick.

It cures what ails you!

This is the perfect drink to help one warm up on a cold day. While enjoying this beverage I recommend curling up with a blanket, a book, a movie, or find someone to engage in good conversation.

Cheese Crackers

¼ pound room temperature butter

1 cup grated parmesan or cheddar cheese

1/2 teaspoon salt

½ teaspoon granulated garlic

1 and ¼ cups all-purpose flour

In a mixing bowl cream the butter for a minute or two at low speed.

Blend in the cheese, salt, and garlic.

With the mixer still on low, add flour and thoroughly combine. If dough is too dry, add a tablespoon of water.

Roll dough into a cylindrical shape roughly nine inches long, seal in plastic wrap, and refrigerate for 30 minutes.

Preheat oven to 350°F.

Cut dough into 3/8-inch-thick rounds and place them on a baking sheet lined with parchment paper.

Bake for 20 minutes until very lightly browned.

Cool and serve.

Homemade Hot Chocolate

3 cups powdered milk

2 cups confectioners' sugar

1 and ½ cups granulated sugar

1 and ½ cups unsweetened Dutch cocoa

1 cup mini chocolate chips

Milk chocolate (optional)

Mix the first 5 ingredients in a bowl. This makes over 2 quarts.

For gifts I divide the mixture into sealable glass jars with ribbons.

To make this even more decadent I include a spoon that has been dipped in melted milk chocolate and wrapped in cellophane. I place the following printed instructions on the jars: Combine one third cup of mix with one cup of hot water and stir with chocolate spoon.

I find the spoons in thrift stores and look for the prettiest designs on the handles.

I make this recipe every year to enjoy during the winter and to give as Christmas gifts. It's a healthier alternative to store-bought cocoa and we think it tastes better. It is rich, but delicious. I spent an entire afternoon in the kitchen trying to perfect it. I had my family tasting it so many times that day, that by dinner time they were not hungry and completely weary of chocolate, as if that could happen!

These are some of my favorite creative packaging suggestions.

Trackit Cookies

1 cup butter, softened

2/3 cup sugar

¼ teaspoon vanilla extract

2 and ¼ cups all-purpose flour

1/8 teaspoon salt

5 milk chocolate bars, or milk chocolate bars with toffee or almonds

Preheat oven to 325°F.

Line a 9-inch x 13-inch pan with parchment paper.

In a mixing bowl, cream butter, sugar, and vanilla extract. Separately mix flour and salt before combining with the other ingredients.

Chop chocolate bars into small pieces and set aside.

Pat the dough evenly into the pan and bake for 20 - 30 minutes until lightly browned.

Remove from oven and immediately sprinkle the chopped chocolate onto the hot cookie base.

Wait a few minutes until chocolate has melted and spread it more evenly over the cookie. Allow to cool a few more minutes and cut into desired serving sizes. Store in refrigerator or freezer.

What is Trackit?

When my oldest daughter was first learning how to speak, I was able to interpret most things she said. For example, I knew that "boopies" was her attempt to say blueberries. But two other words had me stumped – "trackit" and "ga-bwee".

The first time she asked me for "trackit", I had no clue what she meant. I quizzed her many times and would hold up her favorite toys or point to different objects and ask, "Is this trackit?" Her frown and frustration would tell me the answer was no. This went on for several weeks and I began to think I would never figure out what she was trying to tell me.

The mystery was finally solved one day while standing in the checkout line of our local grocery store. Suddenly, my little gal began to babble excitedly, "trackit, Mommy, trackit!" She was vigorously leaning forward in the cart and waving her arm at the candy display. *Trackit must mean chocolate!* I was so gratified that I uncharacteristically purchased two large chocolate bars to celebrate the discovery, and we enjoyed a few bites on the ride home.

After thinking about this experience for a while I came up with this quick and easy recipe for a "trackit cookie."

Now if I could only figure out what "ga-bwee" means, the puzzle would be complete.

Perfect Peanut Butter Cookies

¾ cup butter, softened

1 cup peanut butter

½ cup white sugar

1 cup brown sugar firmly packed

2 eggs, beaten

4 tablespoons vanilla extract

2 and ½ cups all-purpose flour

½ teaspoon baking powder

¼ teaspoon baking soda

1/8 teaspoon salt

Preheat oven to 350°F.

In a mixer cream butter with peanut butter and sugars until well blended. Separately add eggs and vanilla extract together and blend into mixture.

Combine flour, baking powder, baking soda, and salt together before blending into mixture.

Form small pieces of dough into a golf ball sizes and space them on baking sheets. Next, gently press each ball with a fork in a crisscross pattern.

Bake for 12 - 15 minutes, remove trays from oven and place on trivets for a few minutes so the cookies can harden some, then move them to wire cooling racks. This recipe should make 24 – 36 cookies.

79

Best of the West Cranberry Cake

2 and 1/2 cups flour

2 eggs

1 and 1/2 cups sugar

1 stick melted butter

1 tablespoon vanilla extract

1 and 1/2 cups fresh whole cranberries

1 cup pecans, whole or ground (I prefer ground)

Preheat oven to 350°F.

In a mixer cream together flour, eggs, and sugar.

Add the melted butter and vanilla, mix well.

Add fresh cranberries and pecans. Combine well

Place batter in a 9-inch x 9-inch pan.

Bake for 40 minutes. Remove from oven and place on a trivet to cool.

You can double this recipe if you want to use a Bundt pan and make a larger cake.

The name cranberry comes from the German word "Kranbeere" due to the flower of the fruit resembling the head of a crane, a large wading bird found in North America, Asia, Africa, Europe, and Australia.

The Ultimate Pumpkin Chocolate Chip Cookie

1 and 1/2 cups butter

2 cups packed brown sugar

1 cup sugar

15 ounce can pumpkin

1 egg

1 and 1/2 teaspoons vanilla extract

4 cups flour

2 teaspoons baking soda

2 teaspoons ground cinnamon

1 teaspoon salt

2 cups oats

2 cups milk chocolate chips

Preheat oven to 350°F.

Cream the butter and sugars, add pumpkin, egg, and vanilla extract.

In a separate bowl combine flour, baking soda, cinnamon, and salt. Add this dry mixture a little bit at a time to the batter and blend thoroughly.

Mix in oats, then stir in your chocolate chips. The batter will be stiff.

Place generous teaspoons of the dough on ungreased cookie sheets about two inches apart.

Bake For approximately 10 minutes. Cool on a wire rack. Recipe makes about 36 cookies.

Cowgirl Cookies

2 cups all-purpose flour

1 tablespoon baking powder

1 tablespoon baking soda

1 teaspoon ground cinnamon

½ teaspoon salt

¾ cup butter, softened

¾ cup plus 1 tablespoon brown sugar

¾ cup granulated sugar

2 eggs

2 tablespoons vanilla extract

1 and ½ cups old fashioned oats

1 and 1/2 cups milk chocolate chips and/or white chocolate pieces

¾ cup chopped pecans

1 cup shredded coconut

1/2 cup dried cranberries

Preheat oven to 350°F.

Line three baking sheets with parchment paper.

Stir together the flour, baking powder, baking soda, cinnamon, and salt. Set aside.

Using a mixer, cream the butter and sugars until fluffy. Add eggs one at a time. Do not over mix. Add the vanilla extract.

Gradually incorporate the flour mixture and continue mixing until combined. Stir in remaining ingredients.

Use a teaspoon for the dough and drop onto ungreased cookie sheets.

Bake for 9 - 11 minutes, but watch them. If they overbake, the cookies will be dry. Remove the sheets from the oven and allow them to cool on trivets for a few minutes before transferring the cookies to cooling racks. These cookies are a bit crisp on the outside and tender on the inside.

Will of the West

Big skies as far as the eye can see
Across the divide
Is a life for me
How long until I am free?

It's the call of the west wind
The heat of the sun
It's the lure of the wild
It beckons since I was a child

Go west young woman
Leave your world for what is meant to be
Go west young woman
Make a home for your family
Walking in faith
With the seeds you have sown
Step boldly into the unknown

The whispers of change
Tumble in my mind
What is out there?
What will I find?

Don't follow the herd

Answer the call

With these spoken words

Go west, go west

Where the wolves run wild

And the eagles soar

The cloak of peace is worn

And the spirit of hope is naturally born

Go west young woman

Leave your world for what is meant to be

Go west young woman

Make a home for your family

Walking in faith

With the seeds you have sown

Step boldly into the unknown   copyright 2025

These lyrics have yet to be set to music, but they came to me while I was baking the cowgirl cookies. I think it captures the spirit of my first award winning book, *Go West, Young Woman!*

Painted Cookies

2 and 1/2 cups all-purpose flour

1 teaspoon baking powder

1 teaspoon salt

¾ cup butter

2 eggs

1 cup sugar

Egg yolk paint

1 egg yolk for each color

¼ teaspoon water

Your choice of food colorings

Sift together flour, baking powder, and salt in a mixing bowl.

Add butter, eggs, and sugar to the mixing bowl and beat until smooth.

Cover and chill for at least one hour. The dough needs to be cold (it will hold for several days in the refrigerator, if need be.)

Roll the dough onto a floured board and cut into shapes with cookie cutters. Place on an ungreased cookie sheet.

Remove egg whites from yolks. Divide the yolks into separate cups, one for each color you plan to use. Mix a few drops of food coloring of your choice to each cup. I like to use several different colors on each cookie. Red, green, blue, and yellow colorings all bake up beautifully.

Note: I bought a set of soft paint brushes I use only for food preparation. They give the best control over patterns and make for a fun experience. If you don't have brushes, you can apply colors with several small spoons. Sometimes the yolk paint thickens too much while applying it to cookies. Just add a few more drops of water to keep the desired consistency.

Bake the cookies at 400°F for six minutes.

Cool on a wire rack. My recipe makes 24 - 36 cookies which can be frozen.

Roasted Cinnamon Pecans

2 pounds pecan halves

1 egg white

1 tablespoon water

¾ cup of sugar

1 - 2 tablespoons ground cinnamon

Preheat oven to 275°F.

Whisk egg white and the tablespoon of water until very foamy.

In a separate bowl thoroughly combine the sugar and cinnamon.

Place pecans in a large mixing bowl and add the egg whites and sugar cinnamon mixture to it.

Thoroughly combine ingredients.

Spread a light coating of butter on a baking sheet so the pecans won't stick to it.

Bake for 50 - 55 minutes, stirring the pecans half way through baking time to loosen them from the pan.

Remove baking sheet from the oven and place on trivets for complete cooling. Store pecans in an airtight glass container.

These pecans make wonderful gifts during the holidays. My family loves them so much, sometimes I have to make two batches, one to keep and one to give away. I look for pretty and creative packages for all my Christmas baking gifts such as gift boxes and Christmas tins I've saved from previous years. Nuts and cookies wrapped in foil and covered with a ribbon and bow are a nice way to say "Merry Christmas".

Kahlua

½ cup instant coffee

1 cup boiling water

3 cups water

3 cups sugar

1 vanilla bean, split open

3 and 1/5 cups vodka

Mix a half cup of instant coffee cup with one cup of boiling water and pour into ½ gallon glass container.

Add the other water, sugar, and vanilla bean.

Allow to cool.

Add vodka. Place cap on container.

Store in a cool place away from sunlight and age for 30 - 90 days.

I'm guessing you didn't know I made hootch!

My grandmother looked forward to this Kahlua every year at Christmas time. She loved it on ice cream.

Candy Cane Cookies

1 cup butter, softened

1 cup confectioners' sugar

1 egg

2 teaspoons almond extract

2 and 1/2 cups of flour

1 teaspoon salt

Preheat oven to 375°F.

Cream butter, sugar, egg, and almond extract. Separately combine flour and salt. Mix all ingredients together to form a soft dough. Divide the dough in half and place in separate bowls. Add a few drops of red food coloring to the dough in one of the bowls and mix to achieve color.

Break off small sections of each dough and roll into small tubular shapes.

Twist the two different colored doughs together and shape to resemble a candy cane.

Place them on a baking sheet lined with parchment paper.

Bake for 9 - 12 minutes.

After the cookies have cooled slightly, sprinkle granulated sugar over them while still warm.

These are festive, fun to make, and a great addition to your holiday cookie tray.

Snowballs

1 pound butter, softened

½ cup sugar

4 cups flour

3 generous teaspoons vanilla extract

½ cup ground pecans

confectioners' sugar

Preheat oven to 325°F.

Thoroughly mix the above ingredients excluding the confectioners' sugar and roll into small ball shapes.

Place them on an ungreased cookie sheet.

Bake for 30 minutes.

Cool slightly and roll in confectioners' sugar while still warm. This recipe makes up to 60 snowballs.

My favorite cookie of the season, family, friends, and neighbors ask for them every year.

Legendary Cranberries and Apples

2 pounds fresh cranberries- rinsed (remove any spoiled berries)

5 peeled and finely chopped apples

1 and ½ cups sugar (more if needed)

½ cup water

¾ cup dried cranberries

Place fresh cranberries, apples, sugar, and water in a large pan on a stovetop.

Bring to a boil and turn down the temperature to low.

Continue at a low boil until cranberries pop and come apart, and the mixture assumes a thickened glorious red color.

At this time taste the cranberries to see if they need more sugar.

Then remove from heat and add dried cranberries.

Cool and store in refrigerator. Serve with whipped cream (gobs and gobs of whipped cream if you are like my husband).

This recipe is a family tradition at our house. To honor a request from my youngest daughter, I make it twice a year, for Thanksgiving and for Christmas.

Crescent Moon Cookies

3 cups flour

3 tablespoons sugar

1 cup butter

3 egg yolks, slightly beaten (save egg whites in a separate bowl)

3 tablespoons milk

Walnut filling:

2 cups finely ground walnuts

½ cup sugar

2 egg whites

1 egg white for brushing the cookie before baking

Preheat oven to 400°F.

Prepare the filling first:

Combine nuts, sugar, 2 beaten egg whites and set aside.

Prepare the cookie:

Combine and stir flour and sugar.

Next, cut in the butter with a pastry blender and combine it well.

Add egg yolks and milk, blending lightly until dough begins to stick together. Add 1 - 2 tablespoons more milk if needed to acquire a soft dough.

Turn out on a lightly floured board and press together. Work with one half of the dough at a time. Roll dough to 1/16 of an inch thickness and cut with a 2 and ½ in round cookie cutter.

Place pieces on an ungreased baking sheet. Spoon in filling, fold, press edges together, and form into crescent shape. Brush with remaining egg white and sprinkle with sugar.

Bake for 12 minutes. Let cool on wire racks. Makes up to 24 cookies.

Christmas Carrot and Date Muffins

½ cup butter, softened

½ cup packed brown sugar

2 eggs

¼ teaspoon vanilla extract

½ cup quick cooking oats

¾ cup finely chopped dates

½ cup chopped or ground walnuts

1 cup finely shredded carrots

1 and ½ cups all-purpose flour

1 tablespoon baking powder

1 teaspoon salt

¼ cup milk

Preheat oven to 350°F.

Grease and flour a muffin pan, or use a nonstick spray.

Combine butter and sugar and stir well.

Add eggs, stirring after each one. Add vanilla.

Add oats, dates, walnuts, and carrots. Stir together well.

In a separate bowl combine flour, baking powder, and salt. Add to mixture, alternating with the milk.

Spoon into a muffin pan.

Bake for 25 minutes or until toothpick inserted near center comes out clean. Remove from pans and allow to cool on wire racks.

Yes, It's My Mother's Fruit Cake!

Store-bought fruit cake doesn't have the best reputation. However, this homemade version is delicious and makes four separate cakes in the same batch. It's enough for you and everyone on your gift list.

4 cups walnuts (1 pound)

1 and ½ cups pitted dates cut in half (12 ounces)

1 and ½ cups candied cherries (16 ounces)

1 and ½ cups candied pineapple (16 ounces)

1 cup plus 2 tablespoons all-purpose flour

1 cup plus 2 tablespoons granulated sugar

¾ teaspoon baking powder

1 teaspoon salt

4 room temperature eggs

1 tablespoon vanilla extract

1 teaspoon rum flavoring or ½ cup brandy or rum.

Preheat oven to 275°F.

Combine walnuts, dates, cherries, and pineapple in a large bowl.

In a separate bowl thoroughly mix flour, sugar, baking powder, and salt. Add to walnut and fruit mixture. Stir.

Beat eggs, vanilla extract, and rum flavoring, then blend well with fruit.

Line a 9-inch x 13-inch pan with parchment paper. Spread butter or shortening on the paper to prevent sticking. Turn fruitcake mixture into the pan and spread evenly.

Bake on the rack below the center line of oven for 90 minutes.

Remove from oven onto a trivet. After 30 minutes of cooling, cut vertically into four equal pieces. Remove the pieces from the pan and turn fruit cake upside down and allow to cool on a wire rack. Peel off the paper and let cakes cool completely. Wrap in foil and store in a refrigerator.

Queenie Drops

16 ounces quality white chocolate, chopped

1 cup creamy peanut butter

1 and ½ cups plus 1 tablespoon rice crisp cereal

1 and 1/2 cups salted peanuts

1 and 1/4 cups mini marshmallows

½ cup milk chocolate chips

Cool cookie sheets in the refrigerator or freezer for a few minutes.

In a large saucepan gently mix white chocolate and peanut butter together and melt over medium heat while stirring.

Remove from heat and add the rice crisp cereal, peanuts, and marshmallow. Mix well.

Drop by teaspoonful onto chilled cookie sheets.

Melt the milk chocolate chips in the microwave oven and drizzle over top.

Chill for an hour or so to set.

Since this is a no bake recipe, it is quick and easy to prepare and a great blend of salty and sweet flavors.

Cheddar Muffins

2 cups flour

3 and 1/2 teaspoons baking powder

½ teaspoon salt

1 teaspoon paprika

2 cups shredded cheddar cheese

1 egg beaten

1 cup milk

¼ cup melted butter

Preheat oven to 425°F.

Butter a standard muffin pan or use a nonstick spray.

Combine the flour, baking powder, salt, paprika, and cheese. Make a well in the center of the mixture. In another bowl combine the egg, milk, and butter. Add this to the dry ingredients and stir.

Place in muffin pan and bake for 20 minutes. Remove immediately after baking. Best enjoyed while still warm.

Hot Chocolate Cocoa Bombs

½ cup quality milk chocolate

Homemade hot chocolate cocoa mix found on page 74

Silicone round semi-sphere food molds

Melt milk chocolate in a glass bowl in the microwave in 15-second intervals, stirring between each heating until melted. Depending on how many Cocoa Bombs you choose to make, you may want to melt more chocolate.

Using a food safe brush, gently paint the inside of the half circle molds with the melted chocolate. Make sure this is done in pairs, as the two halves will be joined together to make one hollow chocolate ball.

When the chocolate has set, gently remove halves from mold. Spoon powdered hot chocolate cocoa mix into half of the chocolate balls.

Microwave an empty plate for 20 seconds to make sure it is warm.

Place the top half of a chocolate ball onto the warm plate to barely melt the edges. Now set the top half of the ball onto a bottom half filled with the cocoa mix. Gently rub around the edge to seal it. The warm chocolate acts as a "glue" to hold the two halves together. Repeat these steps to make as many bombs as desired.

When ready to use them, place one in a mug and pour boiling water over the top to fill it. Stir well so the chocolate casing will melt and the cocoa mix inside is released into the water.

Everyone smiles when they see this easy and unique way of making a cup of hot chocolate – and it tastes great, too. They're a wonderful gift to give to someone special.

My heartfelt gratitude to my husband Bill and my youngest daughter for being my kitchen helpers, and supporting me in ways too numerous to list.

And to you, my readers, who often become friends, I would be delighted to hear your thoughts and feelings about this book, my art, journal designs, and other books I have written.

Feel welcome to visit with me through my website:

nancyquinnauthor.com

Beloved writer Nancy Quinn is an internationally known bestselling author and wildlife artist who has won prestigious awards in literature and art. Her books are loved worldwide for their honest and inspiring content and her readers affectionately named her the "Montana Queen." Her wildlife art is noted for its detail and accuracy, and she is the recipient of two World Wildlife Art Championship awards.

Upon leaving a suburban lifestyle in the metro Washington, DC area to live on a rural mountainside, she discovered a new world of exciting and unusual adventures. Encouraged by friends and family alike, she wrote her first book, *Go West, Young Woman!* which was honored with the Will Rogers Medallion Award. It was soon followed by two other western adventure sequels, *Stay West, Young Woman!* and *Still West of Nowhere!*

Nancy has always had a love of animals and nature. After college she worked as a conservation law enforcement duty officer for the state of Florida. She volunteered her spare time at wildlife rehabilitation centers, bringing their birds and reptiles into the schools to educate children of all ages.

Over the years she has handled many domestic and exotic species, including cougars, leopards, and tigers, and always had interesting stories to tell about her encounters with wild animals. This led her to write *The Art of the Wild*, a prequel to her Montana adventure series.

Nancy has been baking since childhood and has included a few of her recipes in each of her books. By popular demand she has gathered together her lifetime of recipes and notes, and shares some of her favorite baking tips in this latest book, *Nancy Quinn's Kitchen*.

She resides with her family and pets in rural Montana where she continues to write, paint, practice interior decorating, develop fashion designs, and create new recipes in her kitchen, all while living in the still wild west.

Recipe Index

Banana Bread, 42
Best of the West Cranberry Cake, 80
Better Batter Pecan Cake, 30
Bourbon Pecan Pie, 47
Candy Cane Cookies, 93
Carrot Cake, 26
Cheddar Muffins, 102
Cheese Crackers, 73
Chocolate Almond Bars, 18
Chocolate Brownies, 36
Chocolate Chip Cookies, 48
Christmas Carrot and Date Muffins, 99
Cinnamon Honey Butter, 19
Cinnamon Oatmeal Cookies, 52
Cinnamon Swirl Donut Bread, 66
Cowgirl Cookies, 82
Crème De Menthe Brownies, 27
Crescent Moon Cookies, 98
Decadent Éclair Cake, 25
Dipped Vanilla Cookies, 41
Easy Pizza Dough, 46
Easy Wagon Wheel Flour Tortillas, 24
Favorite Strawberry Refrigerated Jam, 38
Fresh Blueberry Cookies, 28
Go West, Southern Cornbread, 23
Homemade Hot Chocolate, 74
Hot Chocolate Cocoa Bombs, 103
Hot Toddy, 72
Ice Cream Cookies, 40
Kahlua, 92
Legendary Cranberries and Apples, 96
Leopard Bark, 37
Life-Changing Cookies, 44
Luscious Lemon Bars, 16
Milk Chocolate Chunk Cookies, 60

This mug and the apron pictured in the introduction are gifts I will always cherish.

Montana Gold Bars, 62
Painted Cookies, 89
Perfect Peanut Butter Cookies, 78
Presentation Pumpkin Cake, 65
Pumpkin Bread, 58
Pumpkin Cheesecake, 59
Pumpkin waffles, 20
Queenie Drops, 101
Roasted Cinnamon Pecans, 90
Snowballs, 94
The Ultimate Pumpkin Chocolate Chip Cookie, 81
Trackit Cookies, 76
Vanilla Cranberry Muffins, 64
Yes, It's My Mother's Fruit Cake!, 100

Notes

Notes

Notes